Noël Coward's

Brief Encounter

Adapted for the stage by Emma Rice

Adapted from the play *Still Life* and the screenplay
of *Brief Encounter*, both by Noël Coward

T0353534

methuen | drama

LONDON • NEW YORK • OXFORD • NEW DELHI • SYDNEY

METHUEN DRAMA
Bloomsbury Publishing Plc
50 Bedford Square, London, WC1B 3DP, UK

BLOOMSBURY, METHUEN DRAMA and the Methuen Drama logo are
trademarks of Bloomsbury Publishing Plc

This adaptation of *Brief Encounter* first published 2013
This edition with a revised foreword and a new cover published 2018

A catalogue record for this book is available from the British Library.

A catalog record for this book is available from the Library of Congress.

ISBN: PB: 978-1-3500-8357-8
ePDF: 978-1-3500-8358-5
eBook: 978-1-3500-8360-8

Series: Modern Plays

Typeset by Mark Heslington Ltd, Scarborough, North Yorkshire

To find out more about our authors and books visit *www.bloomsbury.com*
and sign up for our *newsletters*.

Foreword

January 2018

It is 10 years since I first adapted and created this version of Noël Coward's *Brief Encounter*. I gasp for air as I look back and realise how much has changed in this time. Politics have polarized, society has shifted and my own understanding of the world has both grown and been challenged. Some things, however, remain deeply rooted and reassuring; the profound power of *Brief Encounter* is one of them. It is with great pride and joy that I return to this life-changing project and, in spite of all the changes in the world, my words from 2008 still ring as true as ever. And so, I will leave you with Noël Coward and my younger self in the knowledge that this great piece continues to endure with passion, truth and hope.

Here's to that!

ER

January 2008

> I love romance.
> I also love folk tales.

Brief Encounter has surprisingly embraced both these passions. In *Still Life*, later to become *Brief Encounter*, Noël Coward wrote a play about an affair. Not a sordid affair but a love affair between two married people. An impossible affair, a painful affair, an unacceptable affair. It is written with such empathy, such observation and such tender agony. This man knew what he was writing about. Imagine being gay in the 1930s and you begin to understand *Brief Encounter*. Imagine the impossibility of expressing the most fundamental of human needs and emotions. Imagine the enforced shame, lies and deceit. Imagine the frustration, imagine the loss and imagine the anger. Each of these emotions is delicately and Britishly traced through the meetings of our lovers.

They experience a micro marriage, a relationship from beginning to end in a few short hours – and how many of us cannot relate to this careful and painful liaison? Not many, I'm sure. Can many of us go through a lifetime without meeting someone and feeling a spark of recognition that we shouldn't, an attraction that goes beyond the physical? And what a terrible world it would be if our emotions and spirits and psyches were amputated at the altar.

And here is where real life ends and folk tales begin.

In the language of stories, we are able to examine the bargains that human beings make. We see how we make bargains with the deep needs of the 'self' for various reasons. These reasons will be familiar to us all: the fear of being alone or of being excluded from 'normal' life. In the language of folk stories the price of this bargain is often physical. A part of the body is chopped off – a hand (*The Handless Maiden*) or feet (*The Red Shoes*). We literally cut a part of ourselves off in order to conform or to be accepted. In *Brief Encounter*, both our lovers have chopped off part of themselves. It is delicately referred to, but Laura talks of swimming wild and free and of playing the piano. Both of these are forms of personal expression – not pleasing anyone but exploring the deep waters of the soul. Alec turns into a child when he talks of his passions, and fears that Laura will be bored. These are people trapped by the bargains that they have freely made – they have bargained their inner lives for stability, family and love. Oh yes, love. I don't for a moment believe that their marriages are all bad or that they are in any way victims. Presumably, their respective partners are as equally trapped by their own bargains and by the rules of society itself. None of us are victims, but we can review the bargains we make and sometimes, sometime, we can escape in a profound way.

I have been reading many Selkie stories whilst making this piece. In these stories, a fisherman falls in love with a Selkie – or Seal Woman – whom he sees dancing on the rocks having slipped out of her sealskin. She too, falls for him. He takes her home and hides her skin. He cares for her and she for him; they have children and live a life of contentment. One day, she finds her old skin in a cupboard. She washes and dresses the children, kisses them goodbye, puts on her sealskin and dives back into the sea. She never returns but sometimes the children will see a beautiful seal swimming far out at sea. This teaches us about our true self. No matter how much we try to repress our feelings or how much we wish to conform, our true self will always emerge. There can be no happily ever after until this true self, or nature, has been accepted and embraced. In the language of folk tales, in order to find one's true self, it is often vital that there is a near-death experience before our heroes and heroines can begin to heal and to re-form. In *Sleeping Beauty* and *Snow White* our heroines are unconscious, almost dead, for long periods of time. In *Brief Encounter* our lovers also die spiritually when they part. 'I never want to feel anything again,' says Laura. This deep depression is an essential part of the process of change. It is something to be endured, understood and then moved away from. The end of the affair is not the end of hope or of love. It is part of the process of change. Alec will travel and see the world in a wider context. Laura will have to re-imagine herself, not just as a 'respectable wife and mother' but as a person in her own right.

My hope is that, like the Seal Woman, Alec and Laura escape. Not with each other in an idealistic romantic way but an escape provoked by the personal awakening they felt when they met. We humans are fearful by nature – it is often somebody else who provides the catalyst for change but they are not the cause. Change can only happen from within. After our story ends, I like to think that our lovers will change. I imagine that Alec will make a real difference in Africa and find an expanse of spirit that seems untouchable in our story. I hope and dream that Laura will take up the piano again and perform on the world's greatest and most awe-inspiring stages.

As I write this, I wonder if these are, in fact, my dreams? That is the power of a great and enduring story; we can all own it, feel it and find something of ourselves within it.

Emma Rice

Brief Encounter

David Pugh & Dafydd Rogers and Cineworld presented Kneehigh's production of Noël Coward's *Brief Encounter*, adapted by Emma Rice, at the Cinema Haymarket on 2 February 2008 with the following cast:

Beryl Waters	Amanda Lawrence/ Dorothy Atkinson
Laura Jesson	Naomi Frederick
Myrtle Bagot	Tamzin Griffin
Stanley	Stuart McLoughlin
Alec Harvey	Tristan Sturrock
Fred Jesson/Albert Godby	Andy Williams
Ensemble	Adam Randall; Jess Murphy/ Avye Leventis
Musicians	Adam Pleeth and Ian Ross/ Eddy Jay

Director	Emma Rice
Designer	Neil Murray
Lighting Designer	Malcolm Rippeth
Composer	Stu Barker
Projection Designers	Gemma Carrington and Jon Driscoll
Sound Designer	Simon Baker

Kneehigh's production of Noel Coward's *Brief Encounter* returned to the Birmingham Repertory Theatre from 2 to 17 February 2018 followed by a week at The Lowry, Salford from 20 to 24 February after which it came back to its home in the West End, now The Empire Cinema, Haymarket in March 2018 with the following cast and creative team:

Beryl/Hermione/ Dolly Messiter	Beverly Rudd
Fred Jesson/Albert Godby/ Stephen Lynn	Dean Nolan
Laura Jesson	Isabel Pollen
Alec Harvey	Jim Sturgeon
Stanley/Bill/Usher	Jos Slovick
Myrtle Bagot/Margaret Jesson/Mary Norton	Lucy Thackeray
Female Ensemble	Katrina Kleve
Male Ensemble	Peter Dukes
Musicians	Pat Moran and Seamas Carey
Director/Adapter	Emma Rice
Designer	Neil Murray
Lighting Designer	Malcolm Rippeth
Projection Designers	Jon Driscoll and Gemma Carrington
Original Music	Stu Barker
Sound Designer	Simon Baker
Casting Director	Sarah Bird
Associate Director	Simon Harvey
General Manager	Emma Holoway
Production Coordinator	Rebecca Jenner

This production was produced by David Pugh & Dafydd Rogers, Stephen and Jenny Wiener and The Old Vic and originally presented at Birmingham Repertory Theatre.

Characters

Laura Jesson
Alec Harvey
Usher/Fred Jesson/Albert Godby/Stephen Lynn
Usher/Beryl/Waitress/Hermione/Dolly Messiter
Usher/Myrtle/Margaret/Mary
Usher/Stanley/Johnnie
Usher/Bobbie/Bill

Musical Numbers

Any Little Fish
No Good at Love
Mad About the Boy
The Wide Lagoon
Go Slow, Johnny
Romantic Fool
So Good at Love
A Room with a View
Always

The action of this play takes place in England during the winter of 1938–39.

Prologue

As the audience enters the theatre, the world is already turning. Ushers and usherettes show people to their seats and sing romantic songs from the time. The band plays and there is a sense of anticipation and pleasure to come.

The lights begin to fade, the ushers' torches do a final scan over the audience as the entertainment is about to start.

Two people begin to talk in the middle of row A of the stalls.

Laura No.

Alec Laura wait! Laura! I've fallen in love with you.

Laura Yes – I know.

Alec Tell me honestly.

Ushers Shh!

Alec Please tell me honestly if what I believe is true . . .

Laura What do you believe?

Alec That it's the same with you – that you've fallen in love too.

Laura Yes. It's true.

Ushers Shh!

Alec Laura . . .

Fred (*in the living room of their house, in another time and place, looking for her*) Laura? Laura? Where are you?

Laura No please . . . we must be sensible.

Ushers Would you sit down please!

Laura Please help me to be sensible – we mustn't behave like this – we must forget that we've said what we've said.

Alec Not yet – not quite yet.

Laura But we must – don't you see!

Ushers   Shh!

Fred (*still searching*)   Laura? Laura!

Laura *gets up from her seat and moves towards* **Fred** *in the living room.*

Alec   Listen – it's too late to be as sensible as all that – it's too late to forget what we've said – and anyway, whether we'd said it or not couldn't have mattered – we know – we've both known for a long time. Laura!

Fred (*he sees her*)   Laura!

Laura *stands between the two men. She looks at* **Fred** *then looks back at* **Alec**.

Laura   Oh, Alec.

Alec   I love you – I love your wide eyes and the way you smile and your shyness.

Laura   Please don't . . .

Alec   I love you – I love you – and you love me too – it's no use pretending that it hasn't happened, because it has.

Fred (*in a whisper*)   Please Laura . . .

Laura   There's still time, if we control ourselves and behave like sensible human beings, there's still time to – to . . .

Fred   Laura . . .

Alec   Laura –

She tears herself away from **Alec** *and joins* **Fred** *in her old, still life.*

Alec   There's no time at all.

Laura *sits in the armchair and* **Fred** *kneels at her feet.*

Fred   Thank you for coming back to me.

Scene One

The curtain rises. It is early evening in Milford Junction Tea Room.

Loudspeaker   Milford Junction – Milford Junction.

Laura Jesson *is sitting at the downstage table, having tea. She looks exactly what she is – a pleasant, ordinary married woman.*

Beryl *walks to the centre with a saucer and a bottle of milk. She pours some into the saucer then makes a funny kissing sound for a cat. She takes a drink of milk, licks her creamy lips and winks at the audience.*

Beryl   Minnie? Minnie?

Myrtle   Beryl! Come here this minute!

Beryl   Sorry Mrs Bagot.

Myrtle   You behave yourself!

Beryl *darts back behind the counter.*

Stanley *enters from the platform. He carries a tray strapped to his shoulders. He addresses* **Myrtle** *with becoming respect;* **Beryl**, *however, he winks at lewdly whenever the opportunity occurs.*

Stanley   Ey up.

Beryl   Stanley . . .

Stanley   Hello Beryl.

He throws a sugar cube in the air and catches it in his mouth.

I'm out of 'Maries', Mrs Bagot, and I could do with some more Nestlé's plain.

Myrtle   Let me see . . .

Stanley   An old girl on the four-ten asked me if I'd got an ice-cream wafer. I didn't 'arf laugh.

Myrtle   I don't see that there was anything to laugh at – a very natural request on a faine day.

Stanley   What did she think I was – a 'Stop Me and Buy One'?

Beryl *sniggers.*

Myrtle   Be quiet Beryl – and as for you, Stanley, don't you be so saucy. You were saucy when you started to work here, and you've been getting saucier and saucier ever since. Here you are – (*She gives him some packets of biscuits and Nestlé's chocolate.*) Go on, now.

Stanley   All right! All right!

He winks at **Beryl**.

Myrtle   And see here, Beryl Waters, I'll trouble you to remember you're on duty –

Beryl   I didn't do anything.

Myrtle   Exactly – you just stand there giggling like a fool. Where's your cloth?

Beryl   Here, Mrs Bagot.

Myrtle   Well, go and clean off Number Three. I can see the crumbs on it from here.

Beryl   It's them rock cakes.

Myrtle   Never you mind.

Beryl *goes to clean the table.* **Albert Godby** *enters. He is a ticket inspector.*

Albert   Hullo! Hullo! Hullo!

Myrtle   Quite a stranger, aren't you?

Albert   I couldn't get in yesterday.

Myrtle (*bridling*)   I wondered what had happened to you.

Albert   I 'ad a bit of a dust-up.

Myrtle (*preparing his tea*)   What about?

Albert   Saw a chap getting out of a first-class compartment, and when I come to check 'is ticket it was third class, so I said to 'im he'd 'ave to pay excess, and then he turned a bit nasty so I 'ad to send for Mr Saunders.

Myrtle   Fat lot of good he'd be.

Albert   He ticked him off proper.

Myrtle   Seein's believing –

Albert   He's not a bad lot, Mr Saunders; after all, you can't expect much spirit from a man with one lung and a wife with diabetes.

Myrtle   I thought something must be wrong when you didn't come.

Albert   I'd have popped in to explain, but I had a date and 'ad to run for it the minute I come off.

Myrtle (*frigidly*)   Oh, indeed!

Albert   A chap I know is getting married.

Myrtle   Very interesting, I'm sure.

Albert   What's up with you, anyway?

Myrtle   I'm sure I don't know to what you're referring.

Albert   You're a bit unfriendly all of a sudden.

Myrtle (*ignoring him*)   Beryl, hurry up – put some more coal in the stove while you're at it.

Beryl   Yes, Mrs Bagot.

She picks up the coal scuttle and carries it to the stove.

Myrtle   I'm afraid I really can't stand here wasting my time in idle gossip, Mr Godby.

Albert   Aren't you going to offer me another cup?

Myrtle   You can 'ave another cup and welcome to it when you've finished that one. Beryl will give it to you – I've got my accounts to do.

Albert   I'd rather you gave it to me.

Station bell rings. **Laura** *stands and starts to leave.*

Myrtle   Time and taide wait for no man, Mr Godby.

Albert   I don't know what you're huffy about, but whatever it is I'm very sorry.

Alec Harvey *enters. He is about thirty-five. His manner is decisive and unflurried.*

Alec   Morning. A cup of tea, please.

Myrtle   Certainly. Cake or pastry?

Alec   No, thank you.

Myrtle   That's threepence.

Alec   Thank you.

He takes his cup of tea and sits down. **Beryl** *scoots DS to check the milk.*

Beryl   Minnie hasn't touched her milk.

Myrtle   Did you put it down for her?

Beryl   Yes, but she never came in for it.

Myrtle   Go out the back and see if she's in the yard.

Beryl *goes.*

Albert *(conversationally)*   Fond of animals?

Myrtle   In their place.

Beryl *(calling)*   Minnie! Minnie!

There is a rumbling noise in the distance, and the sound of a bell.

Myrtle   There's the boat train.

There is a terrific clatter as the express roars through the station. Tea cups rattle and spoons shake.

Albert   What about my other cup?

Myrtle   You're neglecting your duty, you know – that's what you're doing.

Albert   A little bit of relaxation never did anyone any harm –

There is the sound of a strong wind. **Laura** *enters hurriedly, holding a handkerchief to her eye.*

Laura   Please could you give me a glass of water? I've got something in my eye and I want to bathe it.

Myrtle   Would you like me to have a look?

Laura   Please don't trouble. I think the water will do it.

Myrtle (*handing her a glass of water*)   Here.

Myrtle *and* **Albert** *watch her in silence as she bathes her eye.*

Albert   Bit of coal-dust, I expect.

Myrtle   A man I knew lost the sight of one eye after getting a bit of grit in it.

Albert   Nasty thing – very nasty.

Myrtle   Better?

Laura (*obviously in pain*)   I'm afraid not – Oh!

Alec *rises from his table and comes over.*

Alec   Can I help you?

Laura   Oh, no, please – it's only something in my eye.

Myrtle   Try pulling down your eyelid down as far as it'll go.

Albert   And then blowing your nose.

Alec   Please let me look. I happen to be a doctor.

Laura   It's very kind of you.

Alec   Alright – now – look up – now look down – Ah, yes, I can see it. Now I want you to hold still please – (*He twists up the corner of his handkerchief and rapidly operates with it.*) There –

Laura (*blinking*)   Oh, dear – what a relief – it was agonising.

Alec   It looks like a bit of grit.

Laura   It was when the express went through. Thank you very much indeed –

Alec   Not at all.

There is the sound of a bell on the platform.

Albert (*gulping down his tea*)   There we go – I must run.

Laura   How lucky for me that you happened to be here.

Alec   Anybody could have done it.

Laura   Never mind, you did, and I'm most grateful.

Another bell sounds.

There's my train – Goodbye.

Alec   Goodbye.

They shake hands.

Stanley   Beryl, come 'ere a minute.

The band strikes up as **Stanley** *sings to* **Beryl**.

Beryl   Stanley, I'm working.

Stanley   Just come here a minute.

He sings 'Any Little Fish'.

I've fallen in love with you
I'm taking it badly
Freezing, burning, tossing, turning
Never know when to laugh or cry.
Just look what our dumb friends do
They welcome it gladly

Passion in a dromedary doesn't go so deep
Camels when they're mating never sob themselves to sleep
Buffalos can revel in it so can any sheep
Why can't I?

Beryl *joins in.*

Any little fish can swim, any little bird can fly,
Any little dog or any little cat
Can do a bit of this and just a bit of that
Any little horse can neigh, any little cow can moo,
But I can't do anything at all, but just love you.

Stanley *chases* **Beryl**.

Laura *and* **Fred** *enter.*

Fred   Darling! Thank goodness you're back, the house has been in an uproar.

Laura   Why – what's the matter?

Fred   Bobbie and Margaret have been fighting again, and they won't go to sleep until you go in and talk to them about it.

Margaret (*off*)   Mummy – Mummy! Is that you, Mummy?

Laura   Yes, dear.

Bobbie   Come upstairs at once, Mummy – I want to talk to you.

Laura (*on the way upstairs again*)   All right. I'm coming – but you're both very naughty. You should be fast asleep by now.

Upstairs are two perfect children, dressed in their nightclothes.

Laura   Now what is it?

Bobbie   Well, Mummy, tomorrow's my birthday and I want to go to the circus, and tomorrow's not Margaret's birthday, and she wants to go to the pantomime, and I don't think it's fair.

Margaret   I don't see why we've got to do what Bobbie wants to do, just because it's his silly old birthday. Besides, my birthday is in June, and there aren't any pantomimes in June.

Bobbie   Mummy, why don't you come and sit down on my bed?

Margaret   No, Bobbie, Mummy sat with you last night. She's going to sit with me tonight.

Laura   I'm not going to sit with either of you. In fact I'm not going to come into the room. It's far too late to discuss it tonight, and if you don't go to sleep at once I shall tell Daddy not to let you go to either.

Bobbie and Margaret (*together*)   Oh, Mummy!

Stanley *sings to* **Beryl**. **Bobbie** *kicks* **Margaret**.

Fred   Why not take them to both? One in the afternoon and one in the evening?

Laura   You know that's impossible. We shouldn't get home to bed until all hours – and they'd be tired and fractious.

Fred   One on one day, then, and the other on the other.

Laura   You're always accusing me of spoiling the children. Their characters would be ruined in a month if I left them to your over-tender mercies! Circus or pantomime?

Fred   Neither. We'll thrash them both soundly and lock them in the attic, and go to the cinema ourselves!

Stanley *continues singing to* **Beryl**.

Any little cock can crow, any little fox can run
Any little crab on any little shore
Can have a little dab and then a little more
Any little owl can hoot (to whit to whoo),
Any little dove can coo
But I can't do anything at all, but just love you.

Alec *bumps into* **Laura** *on the street.*

Alec   Good morning.

Laura   Oh – good morning.

Alec   How's the eye?

Laura   Perfectly all right. How kind it was of you to take so much trouble.

Alec   It was no trouble at all. It looks like it's clearing up, I think.

Laura   Yes – the sky looks much lighter, doesn't it?

Alec   Well, I must be getting along to the hospital.

Laura   And I must be getting along to the grocer's.

Alec   What exciting lives we lead, don't we? Goodbye!

Laura   Goodbye.

Stanley *sings.*

You've pulled me across the brink
You've chained me and bound me
No escape now by the crepe now
When is the funeral going to be?
Whenever I stop to think, see nature all around me
Then I see how stupidly monogamous I am
A lion in the circumstances wouldn't give a damn
For if there was no lioness he'd lie down with a lamb
Why can't I?

Beryl *joins in.*

Any little fish can swim, any little bird can fly,
Any little dog OR any little cat
Can do a bit of this and just a bit of that
Any little horse can neigh, any little cow can moo,
But I can't do anything at all, but just love you.

Stanley *sings.*

No I can't do anything at all, but just (**Beryl** *joins in.*)
  love you.

We hear the hustle and bustle of restaurant sounds, cutlery. We are in a busy dining room.

Alec   Hello.

Laura   Hello.

Alec   Would you mind very much if I shared your table – it's very full and there doesn't seem to be anywhere else?

Laura   Of course not.

Alec   I'm afraid we haven't been properly introduced – my name's Alec Harvey.

Laura   How do you do – mine's Laura Jesson.

Alec   Mrs or Miss?

Laura   Mrs. You're a doctor, aren't you? I remember you said you were that day in the refreshment room.

Alec   Yes – not a very interesting doctor, I'm afraid – just an ordinary GP. My practice is in Churley.

A **Waitress** *comes to the table.*

Waitress   Can I take your order?

Alec (*to* **Laura**)   What did you plump for?

Laura   The soup and the fried sole.

Alec (*to* **Waitress**)   The same again, please.

Waitress   Anything to drink?

Alec   No, thank you.

He pauses and looks at **Laura**.

Alec   That is – would you like something to drink?

Laura   No, thank you – just plain water.

Alec (*to* **Waitress**)   Plain water, please.

*As the **Waitress** goes away, an orchestra starts to play very loudly. They are playing with enthusiasm.*

Laura   I was forced to play the piano as a child.

Alec   You haven't kept it up?

Laura   No – my husband isn't musical at all.

Alec   Good for him!

Laura   For all you know, I might have a tremendous, burning professional talent.

Alec   Not you!

Laura   Why are you so sure?

Alec   You're too sane – and uncomplicated!

Laura   I suppose it's a good thing to be uncomplicated – but it does sound a little dull.

Alec   You could never be dull.

*The **Waitress** enters with two bowls of soup.*

Alec *and* **Laura** *eat.*

*The **Waitress** clears the empty bowls.*

Laura   Do you come here every Thursday?

Alec   Yes, do you?

Laura   Yes – I do the week's shopping, change my library book, have a little lunch, and generally go to the pictures. Not a very exciting routine.

*The **Waitress** enters with two plates of food.*

Alec *and* **Laura** *eat.*

Alec   Are you going to the pictures this afternoon?

Laura   Yes.

Alec   How extraordinary – so am I!

Laura   But I thought you had to work all day in the hospital.

Alec   Well, between ourselves, I killed two patients this morning by accident and the Matron's very displeased with me. I simply daren't go back –

Laura   How can you be so silly!

Alec   Seriously – I really did get through most of my work this morning – it won't matter a bit if I play truant. Would you mind very much if I came with you?

Laura   Well – I –

Alec   I could sit downstairs and you could sit upstairs.

Laura   Upstairs is too expensive.

The **Waitress** *clears the table and brings the bill.* **Alec** *and* **Laura** *make an elaborate show of going Dutch. The* **Waitress** *is unimpressed.*

Laura   There is something I want to see on at the Palladium. There must be no argument about buying the tickets. We each pay for ourselves. I insist.

Alec   I had hoped that you were going to treat me!

The stars can change in their courses, the universe go up in flames and the world crash around us, but we'll always love going to the pictures and getting lost in the dark!

Alec *and* **Laura** *go and sit in the auditorium as if to enjoy a film.*

The curtain falls.

Front Cloth One

Beryl *and* **Myrtle** *dance the 'Tea Room Ballet'.*

The curtain rises to reveal the tea room.

Scene Two

Milford Junction Tea Room.

Myrtle   Tea time, Beryl!

Beryl   Tea time, Mrs Bagot!

Myrtle *and* **Beryl** *prepare and pour the tea into each teacup.*

Myrtle   Buns, Beryl!

Beryl   Buns, Mrs Bagot!

She brings freshly baked rock cakes from the oven.

They're beauties!

Myrtle   They smell exquisite! (*To a member of the audience.*) Would you like a bun, sir?

She hands a bun to the lucky gent.

Get your chops round this! Shall we indulge, Beryl?

They settle at the front of the stage and eat buns together.

It's all very faine, I said, expecting me to do this, that and the other, but what do I get out of it? You can't expect me to be cook, housekeeper and charlady all rolled into one during the day, and a loving wife in the evening, just because you feel like it. Oh, dear, no. There are just as good fish in the sea, I said, as ever came out of it and I packed my boxes then and there and left him.

Beryl   Didn't you ever go back?

Myrtle   Never. I went to my sister's for a bit in Folkestone and then I went in with a friend of mine and we opened a tea shop in Hythe.

Beryl   And what happened to him?

Myrtle   Dead as a doornail inside three years.

Beryl   Well, I never!

Myrtle *snatches the bun back.*

Myrtle   Here, I'll have that bun back, sir. Come on! (*To another member of the audience.*) Would you like a bun, madam?

Stanley *enters.*

Stanley Two rock cakes and an apple. (*He winks at* **Beryl**.)

Myrtle Got something in your eye?

Stanley Nothing beyond a bit of a twinkle every now and again.

Beryl Stanley, you are awful!

Myrtle You learn to behave yourself, my lad. Beryl, give him his rock cakes. (*She holds two buns up in front of her breasts.*) Stop sniggering, Beryl, and give him an apple off the stand. What people want to eat on the platform for I really don't know. Tell Mr Godby not to forget his tea.

Stanley Righto!

Alec *and* **Laura** *enter.*

Alec Tea or lemonade?

Laura Tea, I think.

She sits at the table.

Alec Two teas, please.

Myrtle Certainly. Cake or pastry?

Alec (*to* **Laura**) Cake or pastry?

Laura No, thank you.

Alec Are those Bath buns fresh?

Myrtle Certainly they are – made fresh this morning.

Alec I'll take two, please.

Myrtle *puts two Bath buns on a plate. Meanwhile* **Beryl** *has drawn two cups of tea.*

Myrtle That'll be eightpence.

Alec All right, thank you. (*He pays her.*)

Myrtle Take the tea to the table, Beryl.

Beryl *brings the tea to the table.*

Alec   You must eat one of these – fresh this morning.

Laura   Very fattening.

Alec   I don't hold with such foolishness.

Myrtle   I'm going over my accounts. Let me know when Albert comes in.

Beryl   Yes, Mrs Bagot.

Myrtle *exits.* **Beryl** *settles down behind the counter and watches* **Alec** *and* **Laura.**

Laura   They do look good, I must say.

Alec   One of my earliest passions – I've never outgrown it.

They start to enjoy the buns. **Albert** *enters with a rose and a boiled sweet. He tosses the boiled sweet to* **Beryl** *and knocks on the door.*

Myrtle *opens the door,* **Albert** *offers her the rose and she beckons him in.*

Laura   Do you like milk in your tea?

Alec   Yes, don't you?

Laura   Yes – fortunately. Do you feel guilty at all? I do.

Alec   Guilty?

Laura   You ought to more than me, really – you neglected your work this afternoon.

Alec   I worked this morning – a little relaxation never did anyone any harm. Why should either of us feel guilty?

Laura   I don't know – a sort of instinct – as though we were letting something happen that oughtn't to happen.

There is the sound of a wave crashing.

When I was a child in Cornwall, my sister and I used to climb out of our bedroom window on summer nights and go down to the cove and bathe. It was dreadfully cold, but we felt very adventurous. I'd never have dared do it by myself, but sharing the danger made it all right – that's how I feel now, really.

Alec   We haven't done anything wrong.

Laura   Of course we haven't.

Alec   An accidental meeting – then another accidental meeting – then a little lunch – then the pictures – what could be more ordinary? More natural?

Laura   We're adults, after all.

Alec   I never see myself as an adult, do you?

Laura   Yes, I do. I'm a respectable married woman with a husband and a home and two children.

Alec   But there must be a part of you, deep down inside, that doesn't feel like that at all – some little spirit that still wants to climb out of the window – that still longs to splash about a bit in the dangerous sea.

Laura   Perhaps we none of us ever grow up entirely.

Alec (*gently*)   I'm respectable too, you know. I have a home and a wife and children and responsibilities – I also have a lot of work and a lot of ideals all mixed up with it.

Laura   What's she like?

Alec   Madeleine?

Laura   Yes.

Alec   Small, dark, rather delicate –

Laura   I should have thought she'd be fair.

Alec   And your husband? What's he like?

Laura   Medium height, kindly, unemotional and not delicate at all.

Alec   You said that proudly.

Laura   Did I?

Alec   What's the matter?

Laura   The matter? What could be the matter?

Alec   You suddenly went away. Please come back again.

There is a crash of a wave.

Laura   You said something just now about your work and ideals being mixed up with it – what ideals?

Alec   That's a long story.

Laura   I suppose all doctors ought to have ideals, really – otherwise I should think the work would be unbearable, tell me.

Alec   Well, every Thursday I come in from Churley and spend a day in the hospital. Stephen Lynn, he graduated with me – he's the chief physician here. I take over from him once a week; it gives him a chance to go up to London and me a chance to observe and study the hospital patients.

Laura   Is that a great advantage?

Alec   Of course. You see I have a special pigeon.

Laura   What is it?

Alec   Preventive medicine. Most good doctors have private dreams – that's the best part of them; sometimes, though, those get over-professionalised and strangulated and – am I boring you?

Laura   No – you're not boring me.

Alec   What I mean is this – all good doctors must be primarily enthusiasts. They must have, like writers and painters and priests, a sense of vocation – a deep-rooted, unsentimental desire to do good.

Laura   Yes – I see that.

Alec   Well, obviously one way of preventing disease is worth fifty ways of curing it – now that's where my ideal comes in – you see, preventive medicine isn't anything to do with medicine at all, really – it's concerned with conditions, living conditions, common sense, hygiene. For instance, my speciality is pneumoconiosis.

Laura Oh, dear!

Alec Don't be alarmed, it's far simpler than it sounds – it's nothing but a slow process of fibrosis of the lung due to the inhalation of particles of dust. For instance, in the hospital here there are splendid opportunities for observing cures and making notes, due to the coal-mines.

Laura You suddenly look much younger.

Alec Do I?

Laura Almost like a little boy.

Alec What made you say that?

Laura I don't know – yes, I do.

Alec Tell me.

There is the sound of a bell.

Laura There's your train.

Alec Yes.

Laura You mustn't miss it.

Alec No.

Laura What's the matter?

Alec Nothing – nothing at all.

Laura It's been so very nice – I've enjoyed my afternoon enormously.

Alec I'm so glad – so have I. I apologise for boring you with those long medical words –

Laura I feel dull and stupid, not to be able to understand more.

Alec Shall I see you again?

There is the sound of a train approaching.

Laura It's the other platform, isn't it? You'll have to run. Don't worry about me – mine's due in a few minutes.

Alec   Shall I see you again?

Laura   Of course – perhaps you could come over to Ketchworth one Sunday. It's rather far, I know, but we should be delighted to see you.

Alec   Please – Please – next Thursday – the same time –

Laura   No – I can't possibly – I –

Alec   Please –

Laura   You'll miss your train! Run –

Alec   Goodbye.

The train is heard drawing to a standstill. The whistle blows.

Laura   I'll be there!

Alec   Thank you.

The company sing the theme from Rachmaninov Piano Concerto No. 2.

Alec *and the train depart.*

Myrtle   It will end in tears.

She sings 'No Good at Love'.

I am no good at love.
My heart should be wise and free.
I kill the unfortunate golden goose,
Whoever it may be.
With over-articulate tenderness
And too much intensity.
I am no good at love.

Beryl *and* **Stanley** *sing.*

She is no good at love.
Her heart should be wise and free.
She kills the golden goose,
Whoever it may be.
With over-articulate tenderness
And too much intensity.

Myrtle *sings.*

I am no good at love.
When my easy heart I yield
Wild words come tumbling from my mouth
Which should have stayed concealed;
And my jealousy turns a bed of bliss
Into a battlefield.
I am no good at love.
I am no good at love.
I betray it with little sins.
I feel the misery of the end
The moment it begins
And the bitterness of the last goodbye
Is the bitterness that wins.

Myrtle, **Beryl** *and* **Stanley** *sing.*

Ah, ah, ah, ah
She is no good at love.
She betrays it with little sins.
She feels the misery of the end
The moment it begins
And the bitterness of the last goodbye
Is the bitterness that wins.
And the bitterness of the last goodbye
Is the bitterness that wins.

Myrtle   I am no good at love.

She exits.

We are in the Jessons' sitting room.

Laura *enters her home.* **Fred** *is holding* **Bobbie**.

Laura   Fred, what's the matter?

Fred   It's all right, old girl, but you must stay calm and try not to be upset.

Laura   What is it? What's wrong?

Fred   It's Bobbie – he was hit by a car on the way home from school . . .

Laura *gives a little cry, flings down her handbag and runs up to* **Bobbie**.

Fred   It's not serious – he was just grazed by the mudguard but it knocked him against the curb and he's got slight concussion –

It's all right, Lau Lau – nothing to worry about – he'll be right as rain in a few hours.

Laura   You're sure – you're sure it's not serious?

Fred   Quite sure – but it was a very lucky escape. The doctor's given him a little sedative and advises keeping him at home for a few days. It must have been a bit of a shock and his right arm is rather badly bruised.

Bobbie   It hurts, Mummy.

Laura   It's all right darling, it will be all right.

Laura *lies* **Bobbie** *down. She sings gently a part of 'The Wide Lagoon'.*

And lovely beyond belief
The dazzling surf on the outer reef
Murmurs its timeless lullaby.

Bobbie *repeats the last line.*

Murmurs its timeless lullaby.

Fred *picks up the paper and starts to do the crossword.*

Laura   Fred . . .

Fred   Yes –

Laura   I had lunch with a strange man today and he took me to the pictures.

Fred   Good for you.

Laura   He's awfully nice – he's a doctor . . .

Fred   A very noble profession . . . It was Richard III who said 'My kingdom for a horse' wasn't it?

Laura   Yes, dear.

Fred   Well all I can say is that I wish he hadn't – it ruins everything.

Laura   I thought perhaps we might ask him over to dine one evening . . .

Fred   Richard III?

Laura   Doctor Harvey.

Fred   Must it be dinner?

Laura   You're never at home for lunch.

Fred   Exactly.

Laura *starting to laugh, almost hysterically . . .*

Laura   Oh, Fred.

Fred   What on earth's the matter?

Laura   It's nothing – it's only that . . .

She breaks off and goes on laughing helplessly.

Laura   Oh, Fred . . .

Fred   I really don't see what's so terribly funny.

Laura   I do – it's all right, darling, I'm not laughing at you – I'm laughing at me, I'm the one that's funny – I'm an absolute idiot – worrying myself about things that don't really exist, making mountains out of molehills . . .

Fred   I told you when you came in that it was nothing to worry about – there was no need for you to get into such a state . . .

Laura   No – I see that now – I really do . . .

She goes on laughing as the curtain falls.

Front Cloth Two

Beryl *sings 'Mad About the Boy'.*

Mad about the boy,
It's pretty funny but I'm mad about the boy.
He has a gay appeal
That makes me feel
There may be something sad about the boy.
Walking down the street,
His eyes look out at me from people that I meet.
I can't believe it's true
But when I'm blue
In some strange way I'm glad about the boy.
I'm hardly sentimental,
Love isn't so sublime.
I have to pay my rental
And I can't afford to waste much time.
How I should enjoy
Were he to treat me like a plaything or a toy,
I'd give my all to him
And crawl to him
So help me God, I'm mad about the boy.

Myrtle   Beryl! Don't you be so soft!

Beryl   Sorry, Mrs Bagot.

Myrtle   Go on.

The curtain rises.

Scene Three

Laura *is sitting alone at the station café. She looks at her watch.*

Myrtle   Can I help you with anything else?

Laura   No, thank you, I'm just waiting for someone.

Myrtle *bends over; she loudly and strongly shovels coal.* **Albert**
enters and, perceiving her slightly vulnerable position, tiptoes

towards her. He slaps her on the behind – she springs to her feet.

Myrtle   Albert Godby, how dare you!

Albert   I couldn't resist it.

Myrtle   I'll trouble you to keep your hands to yourself.

Albert   You're blushing – you look wonderful when you're angry, like an avenging angel.

Myrtle   I'll give you 'avenging angel' – coming in here taking liberties.

Albert   I didn't think, after what you said last Monday, you'd object to a little slap.

Myrtle   Never you mind about last Monday – I'm on duty now. A nice thing if Mr Saunders had happened to be looking through the window.

Albert   If Mr Saunders is in the 'abit of looking through windows, well, maybe it's time he saw something worth looking at.

Myrtle   You ought to be ashamed of yourself!

Albert (*singing*)   "I'm twenty-one today – I'm twenty-one today."

Myrtle   Don't make such a noise – they'll hear you on the platform.

Albert (*singing*)   "Picture you upon my knee, and tea for two and . . ."

Myrtle   Now look here, Albert Godby – once and for all, will you behave yourself!

Albert   It's all your fault, anyway.

Myrtle   I'm sure I don't know to what you're referring.

Albert   I was thinking about tonight –

Myrtle   If you don't learn to behave yourself there won't be a tonight – or any other night, either –

Albert (*singing*)   "Spring is coming and I'm in love again
. . ."

Myrtle   Will you hold your noise?

Albert   Give us a kiss.

Myrtle   I'll do no such thing.

Albert   Just a quick one – across the counter.

He grabs her arm across the counter.

Myrtle   Albert, stop it!

Albert   Ah, come on – be a love.

Myrtle   Let go of me this minute.

Albert   Just a quick one.

*They scuffle for a moment, upsetting a neat pile of cakes on to
the floor.*

Myrtle   Now look at me Banburys – all over the floor.

Albert *bends down to pick them up.* **Stanley** *enters.*

Stanley   Just in time – or born in the vestry.

Myrtle   You shut your mouth and help Mr Godby pick up
them cakes.

Stanley   Anything to oblige. (*He helps* **Albert**.) Where's
Beryl?

Albert   Love's young dream!

Myrtle   Never you mind about Beryl; you should be on
Number Four, and well you know it.

Stanley   There's been a run on the Cadbury's nut milk this
afternoon! I shall need some more.

Myrtle   How many have you got left?

Stanley   Only three.

Myrtle   Take six more then, and don't forget to mark 'em down.

Stanley   Righto. Beryl? Beryl?

He exits.

Albert   It is all right about tonight, isn't it?

Myrtle   I'll think about it.

Albert   It's Claudette Colbert, you know.

Myrtle   Fat chance I shall get of enjoying Claudette Colbert with you hissing in me ear all the time.

Albert   I'll be as good as gold.

Beryl *enters.*

Beryl (*taking off her hat and coat*)   Mr Saunders wants you, Mr Godby.

Albert   What for?

Beryl   I don't know.

Myrtle   You'd better go, Albert; you know what he is.

Albert   I know 'e's a bloody fool, if that's what you mean.

Myrtle   Be quiet, Albert – in front of Beryl.

Beryl   Don't mind me.

Myrtle   Go on – finish up your tea.

Albert   No peace for the wicked –

Myrtle   Go on!

Albert *goes.*

Two soldiers enter, **Bill** *and* **Johnnie***.*

They are blown on by a strong wind.

Bill   Afternoon, ladies.

Myrtle (*grandly*)   Good afternoon.

We hear 'Spitfire' planes flying overhead.

Bill   A couple of splashes, please.

Myrtle   I'm very sorry but it's out of hours.

Johnnie   Come on, lady – you've got a kind face.

Myrtle   That's neither here nor there.

Bill   Just sneak us a couple under cover of them poor old Banburys.

Myrtle   Them Banburys were fresh this morning, and I shall do no such thing.

Bill   Come on, be a sport.

Johnnie   Nobody'd know.

Myrtle   I'm very sorry, I'm sure, but it's against the rules.

Bill   You could just pop it into a couple of teacups.

Myrtle   You're asking me to break the law, young man.

Johnnie   I think I've got a cold coming on – we've been mucking about at the Butts all day – you can't afford to let the army catch cold, you know.

Myrtle   You can have as much as you like after six o'clock.

Johnnie   His throat's like a parrot's cage – listen!

Bill   Gimme a whisky, gimme a whisky.

Myrtle   Get on with you.

Johnnie   You wouldn't like anything nasty to 'appen in your posh buffay –

Myrtle   May licence does not permit me to serve alcohol out of hours – and that's final!

Johnnie   We're soldiers we are – willing to lay down our lives for you – and you grudge us one wee splash –

Myrtle   You wouldn't want to get me into trouble, now would you?

Bill   Give us a chance, lady, that's all – just give us a chance!

He roars with laughter.

Myrtle   Beryl, ask Mr Godby to come 'ere for a moment, will you?

Beryl   Yes, Mrs Bagot.

She comes out from behind the counter and goes on to the platform.

Bill   Who's 'e when e's at home?

Myrtle   You'll soon see – coming in here cheeking me.

Johnnie   Now then, now then – naughty naughty –

Myrtle   Kaindly be quiet!

Bill   Shut up, Johnnie.

Johnnie   Come on lady, what about them drinks?

Myrtle   I've already told you I can't serve alcoholic refreshment out of hours.

Johnnie   Come off it, mother, be a pal!

Myrtle (*losing her temper*)   I'll give you mother, you saucy upstart –

Bill   Who are you calling an upstart!

Myrtle   You – and I'll trouble you to get out of here double quick – disturbing the customers and making a nuisance of yourselves.

Johnnie   'Ere, where's the fire – where's the fire!

Albert *enters, followed by* **Beryl**.

Albert   What's going on in 'ere!

Myrtle   Mr Godby, these gentlemen are annoying me.

Bill   We 'aven't done anything.

Johnnie   All we did was ask for a couple of drinks –

Myrtle   They insulted me, Mr Godby.

Johnnie   We never did nothing of the sort – just 'aving a joke, that's all.

Albert   'Op it, both of you.

Bill   We've got a right to stay 'ere as long as we like.

Albert   You 'eard what I said – 'op it!

Johnnie   What is this, a free country or a bloody Sunday school?

Albert (*firmly*)   I checked your passes at the gate – your train's due in a minute – Number Two platform – 'op it!

Johnnie   Look 'ere, now –

Bill   Come on Johnnie don't argue with the poor ol' basket.

Albert   'Op it!

Bill *and* **Johnnie** *make to leave.*

Johnnie   Toodle-oo, mother, and if them Banburys were fresh this morning, then you're Shirley Temple –

We hear planes fly over again.

They exit.

Myrtle   Thank you, Albert.

Beryl   What a nerve, talking to you like that!

Myrtle   Be quiet, Beryl – pour me out a nip of Three Star – I'm feeling quite upset.

Beryl *pours* **Myrtle** *a glass of brandy. She downs it.*

Albert   I've got to get back to the gate.

Myrtle (*graciously*)   Albert, (*She tosses him an apple.*) I'll be seeing you later.

Albert (*with a wink*)   Okay!

He goes out.

Beryl *pours* **Myrtle** *another glass of brandy.*

Myrtle   I'll say one thing for Albert Godby – he may be on the short side, but 'e's a gentleman.

She downs the second glass.

A train bell rings followed by the sound of a train drawing into the station.

Laura *glances at her watch. She leaves the café and makes her way towards her platform.*

Alec   Laura, Laura!

There is the sound of a wave crashing.

Alec *dashes up the steps onto the platform, and runs towards* **Laura***.*

Laura   Alec.

Alec   Oh, my dear, I'm so sorry – so terribly sorry.

Laura   Quick – your train – you'll miss it.

They both rush along the bridge towards the waiting train.

Alec   I'd no way of letting you know – the house surgeon had to operate suddenly – it wasn't anything really serious, but I had to stand by as it was one of my special patients. You do understand, don't you?

Laura   Of course – it doesn't matter a bit.

Alec   I thought of sending a note to the Kardomah, but I thought they would probably never find you, or keep on shouting your name out and embarrass you, and I . . .

Laura   Please don't say any more – I really do understand.

A whistle blows.

Laura   Quickly, oh quickly – the whistle's gone.

Alec   I'm so relieved that I had the chance to explain. I didn't think I would ever see you again.

Laura   Quickly – quickly . . .

Alec   Next Thursday?

Laura   Yes, next Thursday.

Alec *jumps onto the train and waves.*

Laura   Next Thursday.

The company sing the theme from Rachmaninov Piano Concerto No. 2.

A huge wave crashes and **Laura** *is almost knocked off her feet. She looks up and sees herself swimming. She is fourteen and wild – she swims in the freezing water, exhilarated and free.*

The company sings 'The Wide Lagoon'.

The wide lagoon in which the island lies,
Changes colour with the changing skies.
And lovely beyond belief,
The dazzling surf on the outer reef
Murmurs its timeless lullaby.
Oooh, oooh, oooh, ooh, ooh, ooh, ooh, ooh, ooh.
Warning the heart perhaps that life is brief,
Measured against the sea's eternity.
Warning the heart perhaps that life is brief,
Measured against the sea's eternity.
The wide lagoon in which the island lies
Changes colour with the changing skies.
And lovely beyond belief,
The dazzling surf on the outer reef
Murmurs its timeless lullaby.
Oooh, oooh, oooh, ooh, ooh, ooh, ooh, ooh, ooh.

Another wave crashes.

Laura *and* **Alec** *in a boat on a lake.*

He rows badly.

Laura   You don't row very well, do you?

Alec   I don't row at all, and unless you want to go round in ever narrowing circles, you had better start steering. Look at that beautiful blossom.

She laughs and picks up the steering ropes. A big tree branch is hanging in their path.

Alec   Look at that beautiful blossom.

As the branch looms nearer and nearer, he rises to his feet. She pulls the ropes vigorously. The boat sails under the branch –

Alec   Duck!

She ducks as he grabs the branch and is left hanging. There is a loud splash as he tumbles into the water. She roars with laughter. She stands, grabs the branch and falls in as well. They are very wet and very happy.

They enter the boat hut.

Laura   The boatmen think we are quite dotty, but just look how kind they've been.

They begin to take off their wet clothes, being careful not to show too much. It is a ballet of modesty. They are British and ridiculous, but also kind and respectful. The electricity is palpable.

*A solo voice, perhaps **Stanley** or one of the soldiers, sings 'Go Slow, Johnny'.*

Go slow, Johnny.
Maybe she'll come to her senses
If you give her a chance.
People's feelings are sensitive plants.
Try not to trample the soil and spoil romance.
Go slow, Johnny.
No sense in rushing your fences
Til you know that you know
Your stars are bright for you,
Right for you,

Mark their courses,
Hold your horses.
Speak low, Johnny.
Tip toe, Johnny.
Go slow, Johnny,
Go slow.

Laura *and* **Alec** *sit on the upturned boat, their wet clothes hanging off it like shed skins. They sit by a small fire that warms them and dries their clothes.*

Alec   You know what's happened, don't you?

Laura   Yes, yes I do.

Alec   I've fallen in love with you.

Laura   Yes – I know.

Alec   Tell me honestly – please tell me honestly if what I believe is true . . .

Laura   What do you believe?

Alec   That it's the same with you – that you've fallen in love, too.

Laura   It sounds so silly.

Alec   Why?

Laura   I know you so little.

Alec   It is true though – isn't it?

Laura   Yes – it's true.

Alec   Laura . . .

A solo voice sings.

Watch those road signs,
They'll indicate a bit, Johnny
Which direction to go.
Rely on time and tact,
Face the fact,

You're not Brando,
Rallentando.
Speak low, Johnny.
Tip toe, Johnny.
Go slow, Johnny,
Go slow.

Laura   No, please . . . we must be sensible – please, help me
to be sensible – we mustn't behave like this – we must forget
that we've said what we've said.

Alec   Not yet – not quite yet.

Laura   But we must – don't you see!

Alec   Listen – it's too late now to be as sensible as all that –
it's too late to forget what we've said – and anyway, whether
we'd said it or not couldn't have mattered – we know – we've
both known for a long time.

Laura   How can you say that – I've only known you for four
weeks – we only talked for the first time last Thursday week.

Alec   Last Thursday week. Hasn't it been a long time for
you since then? Answer me truly.

Laura   Yes.

Alec   How many times did you decide that you were never
going to see me again?

Laura   Several times a day.

Alec   So did I.

Laura   Oh, Alec.

Alec   I love you – I love your wide eyes and the way you
smile and your shyness.

Laura   Please don't . . .

Alec   I love you – I love you – and you love me too – it's no
use pretending that it hasn't happened, because it has.

Laura Yes it has. I don't want to pretend anything either to you or to anyone else . . . but from now on I shall have to. That's what's wrong – don't you see? That's what spoils everything. That's why we must stop here and now talking like this. We are neither of us free to love each other, there is too much in the way. There's still time, if we control ourselves and behave like sensible human beings, there's still time to – to . . .

Alec There's no time at all.

A solo voice sings.

Go slow, Johnny.
Maybe she'll come to her senses
If you give her a chance.
People's feelings are sensitive plants.
Try not to trample the soil and spoil romance.
Go slow, Johnny.
No sense in rushing your fences
Til you know that you know
Your stars are bright for you,
Right for you,
Mark their courses,
Hold your horses.
Speak low, Johnny.
Tip toe, Johnny.
Go slow, Johnny,
Go slow.
Go slow, Johnny,
Go slow.

*Throughout the song, **Laura** and **Alec** gently dress each other. There is a terrible intimacy and a terrible foreboding.*

A loud whistle shakes them into real life.

Laura There's your train.

Alec Yes.

He takes her in his arms.

Laura   No dear – please . . . not here – someone will see.

Alec   I love you so.

They kiss.

The sound of an express train roaring, becomes the sound of loud music. It is Rachmaninov's Piano Concerto No. 2. **Alec** *and* **Laura** *stay in their embrace. When* **Fred** *speaks,* **Alec** *peels himself out of the embrace and sits in the auditorium.*

Fred   Do you mind if we have that down a bit, darling?

After a slight pause.

Fred   Hoi – Laura!

The railway has disappeared and **Fred** *and the sitting room have taken its place.*

Laura   Yes, dear?

Fred   You were miles away.

Laura   Yes, I suppose I was.

Fred   Do you mind if I turn it down a little – it's quite deafening . . .

He goes towards the radio.

Laura   Of course not.

He turns off the radio and returns to his place.

Fred   I shan't be long over this, darling, and then we'll go to bed. I say, you look awfully tired . . .

Laura   Don't hurry – I'm perfectly happy.

He goes to kiss her but she turns her head.

He goes to bed. She waits.

The days of the week pass – Friday, Saturday, Sunday, Monday, Tuesday, Wednesday . . . Thursday.

A huge wave crashes over **Laura**, *and* **Alec** *appears above her. He is Superman to her Lois Lane! They are at a very fancy restaurant, The Royal.*

Alec Hullo.

Laura Hullo.

Alec I thought you wouldn't come – I've been thinking all the week that you wouldn't come.

Laura I didn't mean to, but here I am. I haven't been inside The Royal since Violet's wedding reception. It's very grand.

Alec Champagne!

*A **Waiter** enters with a bottle and two glasses. He pops the cork and pours.*

Laura Loving you is hard for me – it makes me a stranger in my own house. Familiar things, ordinary things that I've known for years, like the dining room curtains and the wooden tub with the silver top that holds biscuits and the water colour of San Remo that my mother painted, look odd to me, as though they belonged to someone else – when I've just left you, when I go home, I'm more lonely than I've ever been before. I passed the house the other day without noticing and had to turn back, and when I went in it seemed to draw away from me – my whole life seems to be drawing away from me, and – and I don't know what to do. I love them just the same, Fred I mean and the children, but it's as though it wasn't me at all – as though I were looking on at someone else. Do you know what I mean? Is it the same with you? Or is it easier for men –

Alec It isn't any easier for me. I hold you in my arms all the way back on the train – I'm angry with every moment that I'm not alone with you – to love you uninterrupted – whenever my surgery door opens and a patient comes in, my heart jumps in case it might be you. One of them I'm grateful to – he's got neuritis, and I give him sun-ray treatment – he lies quietly baking, and I can be with you in the shadows behind the lamp.

Laura How silly we are – how unbearably silly!

Alec   Friday –

Laura   Saturday –

Alec   Sunday –

Laura   Monday –

Alec   Tuesday –

Laura   Wednesday –

Laura/Alec   Thursday –

Alec   Don't pass the house again. Don't let it snub you – go boldly in.

Laura   All right! – and don't bake your poor neuritis man too long – you might blister him.

Both   Cheers!

The band starts to play a tango. **Laura** *and* **Alec** *toast each other and dance.*

The company sings 'Romantic Fool'.

Like a romantic schoolgirl, like a romantic fool,
She said she loved him, it was true!
Like a romantic schoolboy, like a romantic fool,
He said he loved her, it was true!
She saw them in Paris in an opera box.
He saw them in Venice in a gondola drifting.
He saw them looking at the sea and stars
From an island beach in the moonlight dancing.

They seem to fly like Marc and Bella Chagall, blissful, ecstatic and reckless. They fly through stars and are giddy with champagne.

She saw them travelling so far away
To all the places she had longed to go . . .
To all the places she had longed to go . . .

Alec *exits.*

There is the sound of a strong wind. **Hermione** *and* **Mary** *appear – angels of decent doom.*

Hermione   Mrs Jesson?

Mary   Laura, it was you after all!

Laura *is brought violently down to earth.*

Mary   Hermione said it was you but you know how short-sighted I am – I peered and peered but couldn't be sure.

Laura   I never saw you at all – how dreadful of me – I expect it was the champagne – I'm not used to champagne at lunch – or dinner either for the matter of that – but Alec insisted . . .

Mary   Alec who, dear?

Laura   Alec Harvey, of course. Surely you remember the Harveys – I've known them for years.

Mary   I don't think I ever . . .

Laura   You'll probably recognise him when you peer at him closely . . .

Hermione   He certainly looked very charming and very attentive!

Laura   He's a dear – one of the nicest people in the world and a wonderful doctor.

Alec *re-enters with their coats.*

Alec   Ah, there you are.

Laura *brings* **Alec** *sharply into the conversation. The mood is well and truly broken.*

Laura   Alec – you remember Mrs Norton, don't you?

Alec (*politely shaking her hand*)   I . . . er . . . I'm afraid I . . .

Mary   It's no use Laura – we haven't met before in our lives – I'm quite sure we haven't . . .

Laura   How absurd – I made certain that he and Madeleine were there when you dined with us just before Christmas. Alec, this is Mrs Rolandson.

Alec   How do you do.

Hermione   How do you do.

They shake hands. There is a pause.

Hermione   What horrid weather, isn't it?

Alec   Yes.

Hermione   Still, I suppose we can't expect spring at this time of the year, can we?

There is another pause.

Alec   No, no.

Mary   Well, we really must be going – I'm taking Hermione with me to see the in-laws – to give moral support – goodbye Doctor Harvey.

Alec   Goodbye.

They shake hands.

Hermione   Goodbye.

Alec   Goodbye.

Hermione   Goodbye Mrs Jesson.

Laura   Goodbye.

Mary   Goodbye my dear, I do so envy you and your champagne.

Mary *and* **Hermione** *exit.*

Laura   That was awful – awful . . . They had been watching us all through lunch – oh dear.

They stand in silence for a moment.

Alec   Laura, I'm going back.

Laura   Back where?

Alec   To Stephen's flat.

Laura   Oh, Alec. I must go now. I really must go home.

She runs away as the curtain falls.

Front Cloth Three

Myrtle *enters. She dances the dance of the loved.* **Albert** *enters. He is cock of the walk!*

The company sings 'So Good at Love'.

She is so good at love,
Her heart is so wise and free.
She'll get the golden goose,
Whoever it may be,
With all her articulate tenderness
And so much intensity.
He is so good at love,
When his open heart he yields,
No wild words come tumbling from his mouth
Which should have stayed concealed.
And it's easy to make a bed of bliss
Out of a battlefield.

Albert   Myrtle Bagot!

Myrtle   What's the matter with you?

Beryl *trips on with the milk bottle.*

Beryl   Minnie? Minnie?

Albert   Beryl, 'op it.

Beryl *turns to go.*

Myrtle   Don't you go ordering Beryl about – you haven't any right to. Beryl?

Albert   You heard what I said, Beryl – 'op it.

Myrtle   Beryl, go in the back room a minute.

Beryl *doesn't know whether she is coming or going.*

Beryl   Yes, Mrs Bagot, well I never!

She goes.

Myrtle   Now then, Albert Godby – you behave yourself – we don't want the whole station laughing at us.

Albert   What is there to laugh at?

Myrtle   Albert Godby!

Albert   How d'you feel?

Myrtle   Don't talk so soft – how should I feel?

The company sings.

They're so good at love,
Their hearts are so wise and free.
They'll get the golden goose
Whoever it may be
With all of their articulate tenderness
And so much intensity.
They are so good at love,
They won't betray it with little sins,
Or feel the misery of the end
The moment that it begins,
And the bitterness of the last goodbye
Won't be the bitterness that wins.
And the bitterness of the last goodbye
Won't be the bitterness that wins.

Albert *goes down on one knee and takes her hand. He begins to kiss it and works his way up her body. She is warm and trusting. He is firm and kind. They are good at love.*

Scene Four

The curtain rises. **Beryl** *is alone in the empty tea room. She is lost in her own fantasy world.* **Stanley** *enters and surprises her.*

Stanley   Hallo!

Beryl   You made me jump!

Stanley   Are you walking home?

Beryl   Maybe.

Stanley   Do you want me to wait?

Beryl   I've got to get straight back.

Stanley   Why?

Beryl   Mother'll be waiting up.

Stanley   Can't you say you've been kept late?

Beryl   I said that last time.

Stanley   Say it again – say there's been a rush on.

Beryl   Don't be so silly, Stanley – Mother's not that much of a fool.

Stanley   Be a sport, Beryl – shut down five minutes early and say you was kept ten minutes late – that gives us a quarter of an hour.

Beryl   What happens if Mrs Bagot comes back?

Stanley   She won't – she's out having a bit of a slap and tickle with Albert.

Beryl   Stanley, you are awful!

They fumble and end up on the floor.

Stanley   I'll wait for you in the yard.

Beryl   Oh, all right.

He goes out.

There is the sound of thunder.

Laura, *on another part of the stage, climbs the steps into* **Stephen Lynn**'*s flat.* **Alec** *meets her.*

Laura   Alec.

Alec   Laura! I didn't dare to hope.

They stand quite still for a moment, looking at each other.

Laura   It's raining.

Alec   Is it?

Laura   I look an absolute fright.

Alec (*taking her scarf and coat*)   Let me put these down.

Laura   Thank you. Alec – I can't stay, you know – really, I can't.

Alec   Just a little while – just a little while . . .

They begin to make tender and clumsy love.

There is the sound of an umbrella outside on the landing, and then the sound of a key fitted into the front door.

Laura *and* **Alec** *jump to their feet.*

Alec *snatches up her coat and the bouquet of roses and pushes them into her hand.*

Alec   Quickly – through the kitchen – there's a tradesmen's staircase . . .

He pushes her towards the back door. She scrambles down the steps and crouches there quietly in shock. It is humiliating and deeply unromantic. Throughout this next scene she pulls herself together, puts on her coat and makes her way down the steps.

Stephen   Alec, is that you?

Alec   Yes.

Stephen *is standing by the entrance to the hall.*

Alec   You're back early.

Stephen   I felt a cold coming on so I denied myself the always questionable pleasure of dining with that arch arguer Roger Hinchley and decided to come back to bed. Inflamed membranes are unsympathetic to dialetic.

Alec   What will you do about food?

Stephen   I can always ring down to the restaurant later on if I want anything – we live in a modern age and this is a service flat.

Alec   Yes – Yes – I know.

Stephen   It caters for all tastes.

He lightly flicks **Laura**'s *scarf off the chair and hands it to* **Alec**.

Stephen   You know, Alec, my dear, you have hidden depths that I never even suspected.

Alec   Look here, Stephen, I really . . .

Stephen   For heaven's sake, Alec, no explanation or apologies – I am the one who should apologise for having returned so inopportunely – it is quite obvious to me that you were interviewing a patient privately – women are frequently neurotic creatures, and the hospital atmosphere upsets them. From the rather undignified scuffling I heard when I came into the hall, I gather that she beat a hurried retreat down the back stairs. I'm surprised at this farcical streak in your nature, Alec – such carryings on were quite unnecessary – after all, we have known each other for years and I am the most broad-minded of men.

Alec   I'm really very sorry, Stephen. I'm sure that the whole situation must seem inexpressibly vulgar to you. Actually it isn't in the least. However, you are perfectly right – explanations are unnecessary – particularly between old friends. I must go now.

Stephen   Very well.

Alec   Goodbye.

Stephen   Perhaps you'd let me have my latch-key back? I only have two and I'm so afraid of losing them – you know how absent-minded I am.

Alec (*giving him the key*)   You're very angry, aren't you?

Stephen   No, Alec – not angry – just disappointed.

Alec *goes out.*

There is the sound of thunder.

Laura *enters the station café.* **Beryl** *has put on her hat and coat and is almost ready to lock up.*

Laura   I'd like a glass of brandy, please.

Beryl   We're just closing.

Laura   I see you are, but you're not quite closed yet, are you?

Beryl *takes off her hat and coat.*

Beryl   Three Star?

Laura   Yes, that'll do.

Beryl   Ten pence, please.

Laura   Here – and – have you a piece of paper and an envelope?

Beryl   I'm afraid you'll have to get that at the bookstall.

Laura   The bookstall's shut – please – it's very important – I should be so much obliged –

Beryl   Oh, all right – just a minute.

She goes off. **Laura** *sips the brandy, trying to control her nerves.* **Beryl** *returns with some notepaper and an envelope.*

Laura   Thank you so much.

Beryl   We close in a few minutes.

Laura   Yes, I know.

She takes the notepaper and her brandy over to a table and begins to write. **Alec** *comes in.* **Beryl** *watches everything.*

Alec   Thank God!

Laura   Please go away – please don't say anything.

Alec   I can't leave you like this.

Laura   You must. It'll be better – really it will.

Alec   You're being dreadfully cruel.

Laura   I feel so utterly degraded.

Alec   It was just a beastly accident that he came back early – he doesn't know who you are – he never even saw you.

Laura   I listened to your voices in the sitting room – I crept out – feeling like a prostitute.

Alec   Don't talk like that, please –

Laura   I suppose he laughed, didn't he – after he got over being annoyed? I suppose you spoke of me together as men of the world.

Alec   We didn't speak of you – we spoke of a nameless creature who had no reality at all.

Laura   Why didn't you tell him the truth? Why didn't you say who I was and that we were lovers – shameful secret lovers – using his flat like a bad house because we had nowhere else to go, and were afraid of being found out! Why didn't you tell him we were cheap and low and without courage – why didn't you?

Alec   Stop it, Laura, pull yourself together.

Laura   It's true – don't you see, it's true!

Alec   It's nothing of the sort. I know you feel horrible, and I'm deeply, desperately sorry. I feel horrible, too, but it doesn't matter really – this – this unfortunate, damnable incident – it was just bad luck. It couldn't affect us really, you and me – we know the truth – we know we really love each other – that's all that matters.

Laura   It isn't all that matters – other things matter too, self-respect matters, and decency – I can't go on any longer.

Alec   Could you really – say goodbye – not see me any more?

Laura   Yes – if you'd help me.

Alec (*quietly, with his back to her*)   I love you, Laura – I shall love you always until the end of my life – all the shame that this world might force on us couldn't touch the real truth of it. I can't look at you now because I know something – I know that this is the beginning of the end – not the end of my loving you – but the end of our being together. But not quite yet – please not quite yet.

Laura   Very well – not quite yet.

Alec   I know what you feel because it's the same for me, too.

Laura   You can look at me now – I'm all right.

Alec (*turning*)   Let's be careful – let's prepare ourselves – a sudden break now, however brave and admirable, would be too cruel – we can't do such violence to our hearts and minds.

Laura   Very well.

Alec   Laura, I'm going away.

Laura   I see.

Alec   But not quite yet.

Laura   Please not quite yet.

Beryl's *had enough. She puts on her hat and coat.*

Beryl   I'm afraid it's closing time.

Alec   Oh, is it?

Beryl   I'll have to lock up.

Alec   This lady is catching the ten-ten – she's not feeling very well, and it's very cold on the platform.

Beryl   The waiting room's open.

Alec   Look here – I'd be very much obliged if you'd let us stay here for another few minutes, please?

Beryl   I'm sorry – it's against the rules.

Alec (*giving her a ten-shilling note*)   Please – come back to lock up when the train comes in.

Beryl   I'll have to switch off the lights – someone might see 'em on and think we were open.

Alec   Just for a few minutes – please!

Beryl   You won't touch anything, will you?

Alec   Not a thing.

Beryl   Oh, all right.

She switches off the lights. The lamp from the platform shines in through the window.

Alec   Thank you. Thank you very much.

Beryl *meets* **Stanley**.

Laura   Just a few minutes.

Alec   Let's have a cigarette shall we?

Laura   I have some.

Alec   No, here. Have one of mine.

He gives her a cigarette and helps her to light it.

Alec   I want you to promise me something.

Laura   What is it?

Alec   Promise me that however unhappy you are, and however much you think things over, that you'll meet me next Thursday as usual.

Laura   Not at the flat.

Alec   No – meet me here at the same time.

Laura   All right – I promise.

Alec   We've got to talk – I've got to explain.

Laura   About going away?

Alec   Yes.

Laura   Where are you going? Where *can* you go? You *can't* give up your practice!

Alec   I've had a job offered me – I wasn't going to tell you – I wasn't going to take it – I know now, it's the only way out.

Laura   Where?

Alec   A long way away – Johannesburg.

Laura   Oh, God!

Alec   My brother's out there – he's opening a new hospital – he wants me in it. It's a fine opportunity, really. I'll take Madeleine and the boys, it's been torturing me for three weeks, the necessity of making a decision one way or the other – I haven't told anybody, not even Madeleine. I couldn't bear the idea of leaving you, but now I see – it's got to happen soon, anyway – it's almost happening already.

Laura   When will you go?

Alec   In a few weeks' time. Do you want me to stay? Do you want me to turn down the offer?

Laura   Don't be foolish, Alec.

Alec   I'll do whatever you say.

Laura   That's unkind of you, my darling.

She suddenly buries her head in her arms and bursts into tears.

Alec (*putting his arms round her*)   Oh, Laura, don't, please don't!

Laura   I'll be all right – just leave me a minute.

Alec   I love you – I love you.

Laura   I know.

Alec   We knew we'd get hurt.

Laura   I'm being very stupid.

Alec (*giving her his handkerchief*)   Here.

Laura (*blowing her nose*)   Thank you.

The platform bell goes.

There's my train.

Alec   You're not angry with me, are you?

Laura   No, I'm not angry – I don't think I'm anything, really – I feel just tired.

Alec   Forgive me.

Laura   Forgive you for what?

Alec   For everything – for having met you in the first place – for having taken that piece of grit out of your eye – for loving you – for bringing you so much misery.

Laura   I'll forgive you – if you'll forgive me –

There is the noise of a train pulling into the station. **Beryl** *enters with a torch.*

Alec   I'll see you into the train.

Laura   No – please stay here.

Alec   All right.

She rises and goes to him and embraces him.

Laura   Good night, darling.

She goes hurriedly out on to the platform without looking back.

Alec   The last train for Churley hasn't gone yet, has it?

Beryl   I couldn't say, I'm sure. I must lock up now.

Alec   All right. I'll wait in the waiting-room – thank you very much. Good night.

Beryl   Good night.

Alec *stands outside the café in the dark and sings 'A Room with a View'.*

A room with a view and you,
And no one to worry us,
No one to hurry us through this dream we found.
We'll gaze at the sky,
And try to guess what it's all about
And we will figure out
Why the world is round.
We'll be happy and contented as birds upon a tree,
High above the mountains and the sea.
We'll bill and we'll coo, woo-woo,
And sorrow will never come or will it ever come
To our room with a view?

Scene Five

Alec *and* **Laura** *meet for the last time at the station café. They are tense and quiet.*

Myrtle *and* **Albert** *enter.*

Myrtle   Look out –

Albert   It's only Romeo and Juliet.

Alec   Good afternoon.

Myrtle   Good afternoon – same as usual?

Alec   Yes, please.

Myrtle   Quite springy out, isn't it?

Alec   Yes – quite.

He pays her, collects the tea and carries it over to the table. He sits down at the table, and he and **Laura** *sip their tea in silence.*

Alec   Are you all right, darling?

Laura   I feel hardly alive at all.

Alec   I wish I could think of something to say.

Laura   It doesn't matter – not saying anything, I mean.

Alec Look, I'll miss my train and wait to see you onto yours.

Laura No – no – please don't. I'll come over to your platform with you – I'd rather.

Alec Alright.

Laura Do you think we shall ever see each other again?

Alec I don't know. Not for years, anyway.

Laura The children will all be grown up – I wonder if they'll ever meet and know each other.

Alec Couldn't I write to you – just once in a while?

Laura No – no, please not – we promised we wouldn't.

Alec Please know this – please know that you'll be with me– far away into the future. Time will wear down the agony of not seeing you, bit by bit the pain will go – but the loving you and the memory of you won't ever go – please know that.

Laura I know it.

Alec It's easier for me than it is for you. I do realise that, really I do. I, at least, will have different shapes to look at, and new work to do – you have to go on among familiar things – my heart aches for you so.

Laura I'll be all right.

Alec I love you with all my heart and soul.

Laura I want to die – if only I could die.

Alec We've still got a few minutes.

Laura Thank God –

A strong wind blows.

Dolly Messiter *bustles into the refreshment room. She is a nicely dressed woman, with a rather fussy manner. She is laden with parcels. She sees* **Laura**.

Dolly   Laura! Laura! What a lovely surprise!

Laura   Oh, Dolly!

Dolly   My dear, I've been shopping till I'm dropping! My feet are nearly falling off, and my throat's parched. I thought of having tea in Spindle's, but I was terrified of losing the train. I'm always missing trains, and being late for meals, and Bob gets disagreeable for days at a time. Oh, dear –

She flops down at their table.

Laura   This is Doctor Harvey.

Alec   How do you do!

Dolly (*shaking hands*)   How do you do! Would you be a perfect dear and get me a cup of tea! I don't think I could drag my poor old bones as far as the counter. I must get some chocolates for Tony but never mind, I can do that afterwards. (*She offers him money.*)

Alec (*waving it away*)   No, please –

He goes over to the counter, gets another cup of tea from **Myrtle**. *Meanwhile* **Dolly** *continues to talk.*

Dolly   My dear – what a nice-looking man. Who on earth is he? Really, you're quite a dark horse. I shall telephone Fred in the morning and make mischief – that is a bit of luck. I haven't seen you for ages, and I've been meaning to pop in, but Tony's had measles, you know, and I had all that awful fuss about Phyllis – but of course you don't know – she left me!

Laura (*with an effort*)   Oh, how dreadful!

Dolly   Mind you, I never cared for her much, but still Tony did. Tony adored her, and – but, never mind, I'll tell you all about that in the train.

Alec *arrives back at the table with her tea – he sits down again.*

Dolly   Thank you so very much. They've certainly put
enough milk in it – but still, it'll be refreshing. (*She sips it.*)
Oh, dear – no sugar.

Alec   It's in the spoon.

Dolly   Oh, of course – what a fool I am – Laura, you look
frightfully well. I do wish I'd known you were coming in
today, we could have come together and lunched and had a
good gossip. I loathe shopping by myself, anyway . . .

There is the sound of a bell on the platform.

Laura   There's your train.

Alec   Yes, I know.

Dolly   Aren't you coming with us?

Alec   No, I go in the opposite direction. My practice is in
Churley.

Dolly   Oh, I see.

Alec   I'm a general practitioner at the moment.

Laura   Doctor Harvey is going out to Africa next week.

Dolly   Oh! How thrilling.

There is the sound of **Alec**'s *train approaching.*

Alec   I must go.

Laura   Yes, you must.

Alec   Goodbye.

Dolly   Goodbye.

He shakes hands with **Dolly**, *looks at* **Laura** *swiftly once, then
presses his hand on her shoulder.* **Laura** *sits quite still.* **Alec** *leaves.*

Dolly   He'll have to run – he's got to get right over to the
other platform. How did you meet him?

Laura   I got something in my eye one day, and he took
it out.

Dolly   My dear – how very romantic! I'm always getting things in my eye and no one the least bit attractive has ever paid the faintest attention – which reminds me – you heard about Harry and Lucy Jenner, haven't you?

A whistle blows.

Laura (*listening for the train to start*)   No – what about them?

Dolly   My dear – they're going to get a divorce – at least, I believe they're getting a conjugal separation, or whatever it is, to begin with, and the divorce later on.

The train pulls away, and the sound of it gradually dies away in the distance. **Dolly** *carries on throughout this departure.*

It seems that there's an awful Mrs Somebody or other in London that he's been carrying on with for ages – you know how he was always having to go up on business. Well, apparently Lucy's sister saw them, Harry and this woman, in the Tate Gallery of all places, and she wrote to Lucy, and then gradually the whole thing came out. Of course, it was all most disgraceful. To begin with, I think it was a dirty trick to make such a fuss openly – the whole thing could have been smoothed over perfectly easily and no one would have known anything about it.

There is the sound of a bell on the platform.

Is that our train? (*She addresses* **Myrtle**.) Can you tell me, is that the Ketchworth train?

Myrtle   No, that's the express.

Laura   The boat train.

Dolly   Oh, yes – that doesn't stop, does it? Express trains are Tony's passion in life – he knows them all by name – where they start from and where they go to, and how long they take to get there. Oh, dear, I mustn't forget his chocolate.

She jumps up and goes to the counter. **Laura** *remains quite still.*

Dolly   I'd like some chocolate, please.

Myrtle   Milk or plain?

Dolly   Plain, I think – or maybe milk would be nicer. Have you any with nuts in it?

The express is heard in the distance.

Myrtle   Nestlé's nut-milk – shilling or sixpence?

Dolly   Give me one plain and one nut-milk.

The noise of the express sounds louder – **Laura** *suddenly gets up and goes swiftly out on to the platform.*

Dolly   Oh! Where is she?

Myrtle   I never noticed her go.

An express train roars past.

The company sings 'Always'.

This can't last,
This misery can't last.
Nothing lasts really,
Neither happiness nor despair.
Not even life lasts very long.
I want to remember every minute
Always.
I want to remember every minute
Always,
Always,
Always.

Laura *stands on the edge of the platform. She has not jumped, but doesn't quite live anymore.*

Epilogue

Fred *and* **Laura** *are at home.*

Fred   You've been a long way away. Thank you for coming back to me.

He leaves.

A wave crashes.

There is a heart-breaking silence and emptiness. A still life.

A wave crashes.

Laura *walks to the piano. She lifts the lid and sits.*

A wave crashes.

She starts to play the opening chords of the Rachmaninov Piano Concerto No. 2.

As the music continues, we see her swimming in the ocean. We see her face as she loses herself in the music. She floats freely.

Song and Verse List

All words Noël Coward and all musical
arrangements by Stu Barker

Any Little Fish (music Noël Coward,
from Cochrane's 1931 Revue)

No Good At Love (music Stu Barker)

Mad About the Boy (music Noël Coward
from Words and Music 1932)

The Wide Lagoon (music Stu Barker)

Go Slow, Johnny (music Noël Coward from Sail Away 1961)

Romantic Fool (music Stu Barker)

So Good At Love(music Stu Barker)

A Room With A View (music Noël Coward
from This Year of Grace 1928)

Always (music Stu Barker)